Praise for *The Diaspora Sonnets*

A Ru

"While the sonnet's tr   ession to the
unruliness of memory   .c images slip,
dart, and soar far beyond the form's constraints. *The Diaspora Sonnets* achieves
a poetry of stunning dialectical energy—solemn, broken, playful, prayerful,
and deeply personal."   —Patrick Rosal, author of *The Last Thing*

"One of Oliver de la Paz's gifts is his sense of the book as a whole. . . Amidst
poems rich in details of the resulting changing natural landscapes emerge vivid
portraits: we see the father in his twenties holding a hatbox, later, a gun . . . .
Every 'Diaspora Sonnet' holds this label as part of its title, the pointed repeti-
tion pounding impactfully, each section bookended by a 'Chain Migration'
ballad and a punctuating final pantoum, a reminder of these poems' origins."

—Rebecca Morgan Frank, *Literary Hub*

"De la Paz employs language both soft-spoken and surprising to elevate the
sonnet. . . . An accomplished mid-career poet, de la Paz joins the likes of Diane
Seuss and Laurie Ann Guerrero in pushing the sonnet's form into brilliant
new shapes for today's readers."   —*Booklist*

"De la Paz moves within the tradition of elegant rhymes, pacing, and the
fourteen-line convention. But he also veers off, as when the theme of love for
family members joins displacement, memory accompanies privation. There
is ache. And, above all, a brilliant tenderness."

—Kimiko Hahn, author of *Foreign Bodies*

"De la Paz is expert at grounding each poem in specificity while also preserv-
ing the universal. The result is a collection that resounds as both achingly
personal and wholly relatable."   —*Poetry Question*

THE DIASPORA SONNETS

Oliver de la Paz

LIVERIGHT PUBLISHING CORPORATION
A Division of W. W. Norton & Company
INDEPENDENT PUBLISHERS SINCE 1923

The following originally appeared, in some cases in a slightly different form,
in the following publications:
"Diaspora Sonnet 11" and "Diaspora Sonnet 13" in *World Literature Today*; "Diaspora
Sonnet 25" in *Poem-a-Day* on July 3, 2018, by the *Academy of American Poets*; "Diaspora
Sonnet 34" in *Cherry Tree: A National Literary Journal @ Washington College* (Issue 5), 2019;
"Diaspora Sonnet 40," "Diaspora Sonnet 41" in *Four Way Review*, Issue 16. Fall 2019;
"Diaspora Sonnet 42" in *The Adroit Journal*; "Diaspora Sonnet 50," "Diaspora Sonnet
51," "Diaspora Sonnet 52," "Diaspora Sonnet 54" in *The Los Angeles Review Online*, Red
Hen Press, September 14, 2022; "Diaspora Sonnet 60," "Diaspora Sonnet 61," "Diaspora
Sonnet 62," and "Pantoum Beginning and Ending with a Big Sky" in *The Massachusetts
Review*, Spring 2023 (Volume 64, Issue 1); "Diaspora Sonnet 64," "Diaspora Sonnet 66,"
"Diaspora Sonnet 67," "Diaspora Sonnet 68," and "Diaspora Sonnet 69" in the *South
Dakota Review*.

For information about permission to reproduce selections from this book,
write to Permissions, Liveright Publishing Corporation, a division of
W. W. Norton & Company, Inc., 500 Fifth Avenue, New York, NY 10110

For information about special discounts for bulk purchases, please contact
W. W. Norton Special Sales at specialsales@wwnorton.com or 800-233-4830

Manufacturing by Versa Press
Book design by Chris Welch
Production manager: Lauren Abbate

ISBN 978-1-324-09517-0 pbk.

Liveright Publishing Corporation, 500 Fifth Avenue, New York, N.Y. 10110
www.wwnorton.com

W. W. Norton & Company Ltd., 15 Carlisle Street, London W1D 3BS

1 2 3 4 5 6 7 8 9 0

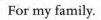

For my family.

But just beyond the house and the meadow
Was the ocean, which you could hear if you listened.

—RICK BAROT

Contents

I.

The Implacable West

II.

Landscape with Work, Rest, and Silence

III.

Dwelling Music

I.

The Implacable West

CHAIN MIGRATION I:
AIRPORT COIN-OP FOOD

My father changed his cash to coins
and stuffed them in machines
to buy us food. The airport noise:
my sense of Father's schemes—

a dense commotion. Gleaming walks
where heels click-clacked—endless
to my childish sense of things. Back
where home was, a blankness.

The streets of Marikina crammed
behind my eye somewhere,
or lost in pockets stuffed with crumbs
of airplane crackers. Where

once a memory, only clothes
shoved in a small valise.
And who's to say what staying close
would bring us? Father's peace?

A way to keep a self from worry?
Or did my father think
about this stack of quarters,
palmed and warm, the sunk

weight of the coins against his thigh?
The sound of the exchange
from one self to another life,
a rattle in the cage

causing the rack of a machine
to turn its gears and drop
a bag of chips, not quite a dream,
but here, for now, a stop.

DIASPORA SONNET WITH MY FATHER IN THE DESERT, SEEING THE VALLEY BEFORE HIM, AND NOTHING ELSE

I imagined him to be god, seeming
to birth a spring wind which rattled

our mobile of spoons. Did he unearth books
to guide us to this moment? And having

read the books—their taboos and their secrets—
did he hide their possible romances?

And did he save nothing in his pockets
save justice and disaster—unpardoned

by the creases in my palm? And having
had his hands framed by a racket of bone,

did the wreck of their meat tell us how
to receive the wild fields? Did these systems,

complicit in however we pushed through,
have answers despite my father's outrage?

DIASPORA SONNET IN EASTERN OREGON, LATE FALL

What was it like? Snowfall and hands in pockets.
An oil drum stuffed to the rim with twigs. Under

sleeping pallets, the crushed apple's insistent rot
and the work as plain as god. We lived and we died.

And when we died, there was the promise of apples.
To clean. To polish. Astringent soaps rubbed on bodies.

To wring out the fact of the cumin-like smell of what?
Of labor? Cider and grease—the hard pits of warehouse

funk. Stink of mattress, stack after stack. The forever
cold of Freon and the drone of fan belt hum.

Our mattress springs idled in the maw of the coolest places
where the red delicious peered over the edges of freight.

And we saw our fruits, forever in the twilight at shift's end.
Stared them down, hard until the red ran green.

DIASPORA SONNET AS A FABLE FOR THE ROAD AND NOTHING ELSE

If the way was written in the dark perhaps it had
steel in it, something metallic, a gun,

a mallet, a piece of machinery—
something cold like the sea, something—nervous

shudders. If our stories were to go on,
the next stanza would snuff out sound. It would

stand in a forest that will not bring you
faith and perhaps a woman carrying a basket

of glass jars gives one to you. Perhaps they hold
dying fireflies. Or, from the side, gleams

the promise of something older than you.
Home? No, the jars hold matches dying

to embers. And she shows you the flicker
of a hand snuffing out the last flame.

DIASPORA SONNET IN THE SUMMER WITH THE RIVER WATER LOW

From here the water's silence bends the truth.
My word for it, silty, uncouth. Our mouths like breezy

sleeping tents—their zipped-up seams whistle gap-toothed
songs. Like bellows. And what hums descends as easy

breaths on watchful heads. We quiet singers held
back by choirs. My urge to cry is suctioned back,

throat cleaned with siphons, notes felled,
then risen as more elegiac names shift to black

with Sharpies. X ashore in a sun-dried coat. X astride
a rocky outcrop, our luggage marred with Xes.

But then there's the world and the truth of where
my steps have fallen leaving craters in brief, clear

half moments. Half notes. Empty mouths of shoes
along the beaches where we wring our clothes.

DIASPORA SONNET IN EASTERN OREGON, WITH AN ORCHARD TENT IN SPRING, AND NOTHING SPECIAL

Half asleep you listen to the leaves of galas.
You wear your best clothes out into the rain

and witness the heavy boughs quiver, the sound
like wasps through the walls of their paper nests.

And the rain keeps pouring despite your need for sleep,
And the sudden harvester light writes names in

red cursive, while coins drop into spectral jars.
Every quarter's ridge is dulled from worry.

You sleep away the light now, which isn't
bright enough to read. The lamps, dim-hued

for the night. You have no words but a name
to pocket. And have known for years, what?

A slip of paper with an old address? Dimes
forgotten in the hungry moments? Time?

DIASPORA SONNET ON THE OCCASION OF MY FATHER, IN LATE SUMMER, SEEING THE GRACKLES OF MALHEUR COUNTY

The desert town is a thousand red shrouds—
a cloud of dust scatters the sun, lanterns

covered in silks, rising with heat. Fields
like faces, open in surprise. The night

encroaching now, insisting on the moon.
I hear a million grackles flock. They nest

above me in the late August sunrise.
I am the blood from a pulse, soft march

against your pillow. I am the marrow
from a bone encased in museum glass.

My prairie exile does not show itself
on any map. I am vapor and ash

in conversation with the citizens
in trees above, more resident than I.

DIASPORA SONNET AS A FLASHBACK TO MARIKINA, REFLECTED IN IRRIGATION DITCHES

Past green on green in flooded terraces,
the onion furrows mirroring the rain

which is a kind of braided silence.
A potential. Across the arc of odd

bright fields, the wind ribbons the images.
It is an intimacy. A man fades

with a kiss on the cheek. His arrival
is the arrival of new light along

the rows. Heat in the marrow. His tender
face and its small nubs of stubble belong

to an air extinct with opacity. Extinct
in the moment of straightening up

to see the horizon. How he measured
himself in the downpour. Mirrored there.

DIASPORA SONNET LIKE ASPHODELS

Even the rain takes refuge: diminutive drops,
sleek, nestled into the pitch of sloped pine boards.

Small contusions—and I blink in the swarm of them.
Because there are no houses to speak of, we will not.

No cylinders measure rain for the garden—no mesh
in the nettled woods. There are no expectations

of this story to revise this story. As when a breeze
snips the laundry line clean and clothes flee

into the alleyway. Ghosts of us, improvisational
and hungry, chase garments past the houses.

We run down avenues not built for us.
The hush after rain brushes our faces,

gathers us in torrents of clothes, tremulous,
while women's voices pierce like asphodels.

DIASPORA SONNET AS A PRAYER IN SPITE OF MIGRATION AND ABSENCE

In absence of blackbirds Father gave me
a diamond-studded sky. In absence of heat,

a window. My dear Father, let it be
lacquered with the slow dust from our bodies

settling the sill. In absence of home
let there be a skein of geese arrowing

past. Dearest Father, you gave me the veins
of grape vines festooning the frame. You gave

placidity in certain places, dust.
You blessed this new place auric with your breath.

Despite the smell of the once clover-rich
field where horses once dwelt, sugared and thick.

Despite the way the landscape chafed our skin,
dear Father, you gave, but I didn't want.

DIASPORA SONNET WITH MY MOTHER
IMAGINING HERSELF BEYOND THE PRAIRIE

I persist in a moment like a solarium.
Window, window, window—sunlit

and slow. A hum of memory. Bee-buzz
vibration of glass as far plane engines

write their misunderstandings above.
I am held by the abandoned lattice

where the wisteria bones form beautiful
cages in their reckless climb up the trellis.

Dear nowhere, I was a girl a minute ago.
I was asleep in the clear chambers of a heart.

I was a secret note in the back of a drawer
sliding forward as you pull the pulls.

I cannot be apart from you, having adored
all these durable moments from which you flee.

DIASPORA SONNET WITH MY FATHER AT THE DOCKS WATCHING SEA LIONS AND SHIPS

Dear homecomings, I miss the humid coasts
where I'd wave at departures as a boy.

Where I'd laugh, startled by the warning horn,
and flinch at the spray, misting my glasses

until I could no longer see the sails.
Here, sea lions pull their bodies to pilings.

Now they sun themselves. They call. Their voices
deep as houses. Joyful barks, familial,

many housed, and many headed. I swear
my rock-ribbed oaths. A word escapes

my mind—ghost of a boat. A ship slides
past the sun-warmed bodies, formal, silent.

It pushes toward the ocean, its prow rocks
the floating families in its soft wake.

DIASPORA SONNET IMAGINING MY FATHER'S UNCERTAINTY AND NOTHING ELSE

On condition of anonymity
we are conditioned by antonyms. There,

the thing made—villainous and ill-tempered.
Repulsive. We're made beasts. Formed from many

scales. How does one love a thing that loves nothing?
Made from the wrack and wreck of you—image

of you, and sent by you to fight your fights,
thus we are all parts and parts. Hibernal

and truant, until your remembrances
have mislaid all the best of you into

us. Tilt our heads, turned this way and that, see
all our old stitching come undone. Our sons—

they see the made thing we have become, hurt
to flinching. The song of skin, soon unsung.

DIASPORA SONNET TRAVELING BETWEEN
APARTMENT RENTALS

What made the grammar of our early years,
moving from place to place, house to flimsy

house, was the meaning made between us, here
and there, and wherever or whenever

we moved. The windows chafed. Father pushed boards
with his palm to make the concavity

recede into dust. The blight in the siding
spoke loudly. In its shape, it said, "Here is

my body." It said, "Here the rain moves across
the rippled wood like a horse through the plains."

My father's words, shaky foundations:
shelter was a noun in sentences racing

past my ears. The verb was family—
the object, swept and scrubbed, leaving no trace.

DIASPORA SONNET NESTING IN A CHIMNEY

We said that love proliferated
the way chimney swifts burrowed into

the old attic insulation. We measured
their generosity and their cries increased.

We heard them in the day and called them
"Our Singers." We could not index them.

Their service chiseled through the dry wall,
and then they'd rush through our living

spaces, owning it all. We had rice. We had
shirts. We had a roof with a choir—

the long gush of their collective, full of thirst
and want. Their calls cut through the ceiling,

the gears of a machine that had already
dug a long furrow into our seams.

DIASPORA SONNET WITH A WOK, A BROKEN VENT, AND NOTHING ELSE

My mother soaked her aching feet because
the disrepair of workdays left her rooted.

Those hours in the broken care of bosses'
smoldering burners. Poorly vented and

oily. Grease-spotted floors. Kitchens, booming
loud with argumentative oven vents.

Her ears went deaf on this continent. No
shelter or cover. No paved road home. No

quarter given. No skin, just bone. *It took
me years to wash this smell from me—fry grease.*

Her skin bore the hard calluses of work.
And I know what else it took—years to wash

the stories from her mind. The months to save
what's left of her aspirational self.

DIASPORA SONNET ON THE GLOSSY COVER OF *TV GUIDE*

Because we were not chosen for the dance
we scouted work parties, fast food. Romanced

in darkened rooms where loudly pool cues stalked
us, angry broods with games of chance. We weren't

chosen for the dance with kings and senators.
We're blades of grass; while luminaries, fat

on roasted pig and ribs on spits, enhanced
their looks with hair products that let them shine

beautifully above us in orbit—
whole galaxies of the gorgeous on TV.

To see them wear such luscious finery
and shine like polished stones for want of love.

For want of having been. And we tuned out
the channels, cycled down, and felt the crash.

DIASPORA SONNET WITH THE RED STAIN OF
LAPINS AND NOTHING ELSE

Because summer resides in deciduous fruit
I resolve to surrender. I kiss gods, engorged

and hollow, armed then dismembered
by pecking birds in their floral, orchestral

gestures. I envy their inimitable altos,
their arduous joy at having. Because

I cannot rival Spring and all its notable
offspring—the joyful violence of men

at the gate. The upsurge of cars along
the interstate. I cannot find a place to hide

the heavy cherries that I've plucked
because I bear them in the smallest pockets.

Luck would have me think of ways to pray
with thanks. Even grackles arise to dance.

DIASPORA SONNET WITH MY FATHER'S STAMPED TIME CARD

My father cannot leave his imperfect
world alone. And so we hemmed his tears, sewed

lullabies to allay fears of alley-
ways deemed unsafe for casual walkers.

Made music sing over the din of razored
talkers. We are guilty of rebalancing

the tires to speed the car past the wreck
of fires from our burned-out neighborhoods.

The tenements bombed out, the stores with goods
smashed on linoleum tiles. We do what

we do and they put it in our files. Stamped
papers shuffled on someone's desk. Father

stamping out the past. It's what he does best.
Calls it self-care. You call it what you will.

DIASPORA SONNET DRIVING ALONG THE COAST

Ghostly boats glide along the glassy sheen.
Some apparitions inside my father's

head. Are they indexes? A tell? A way
to face a futile gesture of his needs?

I spy a migration—a dingy in
the curve of a wave. A shivering seed.

Distracted, he drives past cattle atop
a manure mound. The corral swallowed by

torrential rainfall. All the commonplace
beasts are ushered into their pens. The sheep

in their white suits passing through halls of glass.
Father, reflected in the beading rain,

is elsewhere now. As we move through elsewhere
on this coast, or the next. As far as here.

DIASPORA SONNET WITH A DEATH IN AN APARTMENT AND THE FEEDBACK FROM A RADIO

The planet pulls our bodies through the year.
Delivers us, headlong, into the tears

in currents. The ebbs and flows of blood, in
chambers, bombastic and flooded with names

unremembered. Neighbors borne feet first through
their door arches. Down the corridors, old

and lonesome and lost. Their voices suture
the silence behind them when a pulsing

little song hits a hammered staccato—
EMT's boots, radio bursts, other

first responders—called in because someone
didn't go to work, someone missed their shift,

someone lost a day, and the day, like one
arm then another pulled through a sleeve, goes.

DIASPORA SONNET WITH A CRACKED WINDSHIELD, A SILENT COMMUTE, AND NOTHING SPECIAL

He navigates in silence. I see a thread
of thought shine in the light—held out as two

branches hold the spider's web. His mind,
back there in the black-and-white photographs

where there are no paths to walk upon. Grass
and bramble, trod down by rough politics.

Where we come from, a tributary. Net-
work of nerves. Rhizome of many forks. Where

there are memories, he lets the splinters
of those shards bury themselves deep into

skin. Where there's a past, he lets it drive nails
into a tongue he holds back. Father, speak.

If the roads we take to see the country
were in hindsight, we would never arrive.

DIASPORA SONNET OCCURRING A MOMENT
AFTER WORK

Having listened to the moonlit yard—
having fallen asleep in the quiet

of the vespiary. Having slept through
rain despite rain. Then sudden traffic

lights in a red cursive. Then having
worried the cost of a ride home.

Having worried the coin into a specter,
I saw its ridges honed. Its grooves into

my palm. Having slept, the light was not
right. It was too raucous. Too raucous

for the night. Having known the years
and what they've listened for—

then my breath and its pace with here,
in sync with here despite being here.

PANTOUM BEGINNING AND ENDING WITH THORNS

Because of the way a border on a map twists into thorns
my father stood in line in a ruined country with ruined men.
We were footnotes on charred parchment. The boundaries, lost
at the precipice of a war, shifting on the hour in spliced histories.

My father stood in line in a ruined country with ruined men,
and what for? Did he imagine the desert he would bring us to?
At the precipice of a war, shifting on the hour in spliced histories,
the call to leave home throbbed inside him. Urgent pulses—

And what for? Did he imagine the desert he would bring us to?
Its thirsty and abandoned towns? There was a fire spreading within—
the call to leave home throbbed inside. Urgent pulses
crossed and uncrossed like tributaries on freshly inked maps.

In thirsty and abandoned towns, there was a fire spreading within
so he took us away because the country was ruled by swords
which crossed and uncrossed like tributaries on freshly inked maps.
And the guns would sound all night like feast days of saints.

He took us away because the country was ruled by swords
and men emblazoned with chevrons and pins.
And the guns would sound all night like feast days of saints
but really, there was more silence. There was worry and fear

And men emblazoned with chevrons and pins
would draw black Xes over places they'd conquered.
Really. Then more silence. Then worry and fear.
The flies would sing their hymnals in procession around the dead.

The black Xes over places now conquered.
Maps of provinces, cities, family lines drawn and redrawn.
The flies singing their hymnals in procession around the dead
and my father with a ticket to flee because home wouldn't let us stay.

Maps of provinces, cities—family lines drawn and redrawn
into travelogues and diaries. Into stories passed in the night
like my father with a ticket to flee because home wouldn't let us stay.
Hum of the plane engine. Hum of idling car. Hum of the outboard motor.

Into travelogues and diaries. Into stories passed in the night,
we were footnotes on a charred parchment. The borders lost
to the hum of planes, of idling cars, hum of outboard motors
because of the way the line on a map twists into thorns.

II.

Landscape with Work,
Rest, and Silence

CHAIN MIGRATION II:
ON NEGATIONS AND SUBSTITUTIONS

Not the tamarind. But instead
lemon, though sometimes lime.
Not nipa mats on floors for beds
but rather frames that chime

when running hands through oak spindles.
Never your thickest coat
for winter. Parkas, a must! Kin
sends discards, clothes to float

you through the season. No soy sauce?
No problem! Worcestershire
salts the tongue in equivalence.
No coconut vinegar?

Sometimes white will do. Its sour
flavor pushes us through
the recipe. Sometimes it's our
expectations we screw

into a tighter face. Sometimes
what home is . . . isn't that.
Adjust the thermostat to nine
degrees past. Habitats

don't bend to our aftermaths. No.
There are, instead, some swaps—
a roof over our heads. And now?
A self to lose? A trap?

The gamble of the recipe
is salt and sweat, the wrong
of it. The parts necessitate
a flavor test. Too strong?

Then let's behave, hide our features—
distrust the place and stare
long into the TV's ether.
Lose words into the air.

DIASPORA SONNET IN THE HEAT OF THE AFTERNOON WITH GOOD GOSSIP AND NOTHING SPECIAL

The old men drink their spritzers and gossip
under awnings. Red-hued and blustery,

like two roosters on the side of a road.
Skyward they crane their necks and laugh, sometimes

they wonder about kings and future kings
and how the muscles peer from their taut skin.

Laugh lines or frown lines. My father can't pick
which. His wrinkles pick their own trajectory.

Afternoons lack the luxury of stars.
The heat unreels like news from the speaker

perched high on the refrigerator. Stuck
amid the buzz of insects and static,

the mind repairs itself with sound. Father,
among friends, talks story. Makes himself found.

DIASPORA SONNET ON MY FATHER'S GUNS

My father's rifle is a house of sorts.
Its nerves are blunted, cold beneath the steel.

And rooms echo with reports of noise. Loud
and boisterous hailstones? Not bullets. The thing

we flee from? Rain and nature? The rifle
makes a poor roof. He holsters it to him

in fear of his body and the pains of
imperatives from another country.

The shelter's flimsy and flecked with sparks. Ash
and fireworks on display. July. Dark

to light. The open sky blooming, bouquets,
my father's bewilderment. There are ghost-

lights seared into what had been seen. A weight
as heavy as the gun my father cradles.

DIASPORA SONNET GENTLY PUSHED INTO A DUSTPAN

I see my father kneel in tenements
and public spaces—places where he declares

our decorous hungers. There, the lilies
dry in the sun, breathless. Desiccating mouths

tilting downward toward the red-marrow floor.
My father's knees are bruised as he dustpans

brick dust, ground by many shoes. How the swirls
of grain drift with passing travelers, writes

the script of passing bodies. Whorls. Granules.
Shifting specks making legible faces,

all of whom resemble someone you've lost.
Perhaps, in his sweeping, he is truly

gathering something, as the bristles swish,
sounding like a faintly whispered secret.

DIASPORA SONNET WITH MY FATHER IN THE OFF HOURS

The workers hum to while away afternoons
and tenants chide their sons to sweep from room

to room last night's dust motes—stirred dreams entangled
in wide streaks of light that, in the daytime,

bloom. Unsparing, bright—like operatic
high notes. Pierced and round, the clouds of sleep fill

with sound. And Father, whistling his tune,
leans against his broom to listen to men

complain about their lives and each other.
Brush strokes wave away the dirt. Losses. Tunes

so deep within the brain we cannot help
but weep as sons push brushes past door

after door, locked tight like shut eyes and tombs.
Hear their quiet bristles, their heavy score.

DIASPORA SONNET WITH SWIFTS INSISTING ON THEIR ACCOMMODATIONS

They have such perfect closeness, those birds there,
flying in their spirals, cutting sharply

past the flat surface of the house, then up,
skyward into the stratosphere. They hurt

to watch—and the ways they move, unified.
Upswept, wind and wind, they bank and dive—burst

and curl, their joy at being unwound. Lost
ın a knowing of bodies and bodies,

angled just so. The speeds at which they glide
cannot be known by anyone but these

selves. Then migrating on when the season
calls for it, families at their leisure,

this choosing to in the meanwhiles of when.
How beautiful it is to know the time.

DIASPORA SONNET MEASURING TIME WITH HARVEST PRODUCE AND NOTHING ELSE

The almanac to live in fantasy
paces time with myth and flowers—corn husks,

silken gold in weathered fields, the dahlias,
ornate and temperamental in the earth,

the musky soil, tilled by Father's hands. Blooms
of pears. The odorific tang of bloom,

redundant in the joy of field flower,
tugs us through the decades of here and now.

How we remember the curled lip of a shirt
filled like a bowl of pears. Remembered burst

of blossom and heavy crates of onions,
their acid tang, and what the future asks

and how the decades carry us past rows,
watered and sown. The persistent soil.

DIASPORA SONNET AS A FLASHBACK TO
MARIKINA WHILE SETTING SPRINKLER HEADS

Shush of water splashes terraces. Rows
mirrored in the flooding irrigation—

the reflection, a kind of brimmed silence.
A potential. Across the swath of light,

staggered fields in the wind ribbon images.
The intimacy of a beloved kissed

into oblivion. These new lights rise
along furrows, tender in their tendrils

of warmth, extinct with potentials. Extinct
in the early shift of irrigation,

the sprinkler heads shush all intention.
While a single thought—to stand straight and see

the horizon beyond the razored green.
To see yourself in the mirroring streams.

DIASPORA SONNET IMAGINING MY FATHER IN LINE AT CAMP CRAME

In these moments nothing passing between
hearts, everything turning to mist. Then blank.

In his mind, sleeping wars and the sleeping
soldiers with rifles against their knees. Guns

and the shoulder straps, seductively slung
across the breastbones of the uniformed.

I imagine them standing. In boredom,
they cross one leg over the other. Steam

off their wet brows changes light. Forms them
into light. And morning is a softening

bronze. I imagine Father forfeiting
nothing, save the grace that is this moment.

As my father forfeits field and nation,
imagine nothing in these turning skies.

DIASPORA SONNET SLEEPING IN SPRINGTIME AMONG THE BALES AND NOTHING SPECIAL

If only by some miracle these thoughts
would end having worried my brain as one

who nestles into mounds of hay. The bale
wears its field-smell—its ephemeral mind,

the idea of safety. Worry, the mouth
of a sleeping breather. The instinct to love is to worry.

And night upon night mounds of cut grasses,
a kind of shelter from unmoored stars. Night

upon night, a slip of the moon through creases
between bodies. Bodies beneath thatch. Between

worries and between slippages of selves.
Those of us who stayed awake—we who stayed

awake in the expectant dwelling in flux—
sewn up. And here. Very quiet. Breathing.

DIASPORA SONNET IMAGINING MY FATHER ON THE STREETS OF MARIKINA, METRO MANILA

My father in his twenties wears his pressed suit
and carries a small hatbox possessing something

sensible. Something pleased with itself.
And through the cacophony of the queued up

industry of men coming home from work, my father is plain.
Avenues of dust and motored trikes belch in umbrage

to the poem of it—we might've stayed. My plain father,
tired of the staccato of each adjectival commute:

loamy, worn, blunted, and angry. Plain as the possibility
of wonder in a hatbox. As sensible as the need to leave

the country. He is the center of sense, my father,
never hesitating to thread his Windsor knot and polish

his one pair of dress shoes. Because he will wear his hat.
He will go. And, thereafter, we will live in his thereafters.

DIASPORA SONNET LINED IN FAUX SILK WITH PLENTY OF STORAGE SPACE

The romance of the suitcase is all elegant
weight. The click of latches and the clasps

nestled into their metal fists. The urge of zippers
and the urgency of the shimmery lining

like a false wall in old houses. Where the secrets
breathe in the cortex of their knowledge—

what they know: love. Love is a continent
away. It is chenille, soft and long-suffering

and worn only once. And there are other
more secret wants. Love is in the creases

of this bindery. This mystery for
another place to be opened with all

its irrational promises. Folded.
The brazen collars. Articulate slacks.

DIASPORA SONNET AT THE END OF THE HARVEST SEASON WITH THE LAST OF THE GALAS

An expectant evening of snow like the breath after
a sentence. The opulent clean of a host city

shined like dishes run through the machine—
some days I am almost a man. The year's last

windfall of apples is shined and taken from my bag.
I hand-picked each one, twisting them slightly

off branches. I am not from a cold country.
I am not immune to this spectacle of cityscape

and dream. The way the tin light suggests fidelity
to this small room also suggests I will move beyond

this cold America. And the galas on the sill reflect
a shepherded outcome from these windows.

They bring little light, the apples. What happens then
after the frosts? Will there be polish in the waxen bite?

DIASPORA SONNET AS A PHOTOGRAPH OF ME IN 1977

I see a child dancing in the doorway.
He is a celestial repetition—a comet on

an oblong path. I watch him segment the light
with outstretched hands. The hallway shadows

zigzagging in his spastic delight. He is lost
beyond the stasis of unsent mail, arching

his ribs outward, bursting against the stratosphere
of the housing complex, bright and balletic

as one whose body has been lifted by guy wire
above the darkened theater. And far beyond you

the charts that mark our own departures, forgotten
at least for now as we reckon with your joy.

Dear child, may you rise, wayward, into the sky.
May you stay unified by the light, spellbound.

DIASPORA SONNET AS A LONG-DISTANCE COLLECT CALL FROM MANILA, AND NOTHING TO SAY

What is rooted inside of my throat—an anchor
of long vowels. Glottals like hooks not relinquishing

their holds. How fastidious, the sound at the end
of the line. I am voided by the voice asking

How are you? Asking *Send money.* The air
inscrutable hands making the words disappear

like a cheap parlor trick. I stay silent. I flicker
and flare in my pleas to myself for absolution.

Here is the house where my body resides. Here
is the window that shows the nimbus of the moon.

I hear the outlines of language slipping
its trackless beams across the floor. Over there

it is the rainy season, and we talk about the weather.
How it will, doubtlessly, expose the roots in the hills.

DIASPORA SONNET AT A PUBLIC POOL IN FRUITLAND, IDAHO, WITH NO QUARTERS

After working orchard rows, migrant kids
malinger outside, tall chain-link fencing

threaded with thistles. From empty streets
blacktop heat, thick as pomade on the elders'

dyed-black crowns. Inside, the community pool's
packed with gossip. So many bodies and no room

to swim. I just stand, fingers curled on links,
with skinny kids in overlong T-shirts

leaning on posts, chatting up pool denizens.
And the vendors wheel drink carts outside,

purse their lips and chirp to the kids, summoning
pocket change. I imagine drawing breath

between dips as other kids float on backs,
water, lukewarm. No tide to pull them down.

DIASPORA SONNET IN THE MORNING BEFORE
THE RUSH OF CROWDS, WHEN MOTHER SHOPS
AND IS NOT SEEN

The way I walk market aisles with intention—
my neck, straight. Eyes focused as I enter

with purpose borne of worry. Cereals,
wheat bread, sausages, landscapes crossed over

in a plane. I am flying above the patchwork of
mornings and feeling dizzy. Truly I am

making things up as I scan prices. Morning
into morning into the next. Tiles shined

into parcels of purpose. I don't know
why we boarded a plane many years past—

the plane was there and we needed another
there. I can't tell you much about flying.

I was nauseous. My mind spun, spins to find
what errand brings me here or hereafter.

DIASPORA SONNET AS NOTECARDS WITH NEW WORDS AND NOTHING ELSE

The word home ensnared with thorns.
Gored by. A resident ache in the back

of the mouth. Jaw slightly opened, tilted,
angled to a degree. The air spills out.

But wrong. Lips rounded though not a curled ramp
for the hollow vowel to sound out its bowl.

The tongue back near incisors. Too many
unsayable residences. Too much thrust

of diaphragm. The balletic turn of
phrase to kindred who've not the common

language. Our regard for each other, stuck
in long pauses. Milliseconds into

gazes. The marked notecards pasted over
this and that, refrigerator, bed, door.

DIASPORA SONNET AS MY GRANDMOTHER'S FEARS

I close the shutters, leave a wink
of light to keep from burning down

my paper house. The seams are creased.
I move about in my tattered plight

slowly. Elbow on the table, skin puckered
makes a kissing sound as I lift my arm

to shade my eyes from beams cutting through.
This desert place is not the home I want.

Slowly baking air at noontime, despite
my insistence on shadow—I am hot

in the shade of my dwelling. There are dogs
outside, nosing, and I hear them speak their

breathy language. Their humid speeches break
their deliberations about staying.

DIASPORA SONNET, AGAIN, AS MY GRANDMOTHER'S FEARS

I have made myself small—a ball of yearning.
My skin, translucent drapes I hide behind.

I note my hours inside by angles
of sunbeam. I make my voice so low, hoarse

from whispered names for home. I cannot hear
the words from my mouth, cannot remember

wherever home is. I know it is noon
when the air inside is a breathing mouth.

My clothes, spotted by sweat. Outside the house
loud people, giants in their noise, pass by.

Through the curtains their shadows beckon me—
a carnival of noisy ghosts with their odd smells

and cooking. I roll rosary beads, small
orbits between my fingers. Quiet moons.

DIASPORA SONNET IN THE GREAT SAGE DESERT
WITH THISTLE, PYRITE, AND NOTHING ELSE

My father's paradise is hollowed out.
We live so calmly in a famished basin

populated by the purpled crowns
of Russian thistle. The sage desert

is a dry throat and I am a whole nation
in my dry mouth. The summons

to reside here, to swallow a testament.
From the rock spouts rock and no

syntactical hook, the wide blue sky
does not fasten my attention. Constantly

I am bewildered by miles of nothing,
germinating landscape gifted to me.

I thought I'd own these irrigated fields
instead, this caustic dust stipples my tongue.

DIASPORA SONNET IN THE SAGE DESERT WHEN GRANDMOTHER TRIES TO SLEEP

Without the noise of home I learn
to hear my body's own sound.

It is like sleeping in a narrow boat,
waters slapping at the wooden sides

wanting to carve a space already
hollowed out. The failure of

the body's quiet is the triumph of the ear—
having been pressed to the earth

in my search for currents of missing
footsteps. These feet cannot tread

water. And my ear cannot separate
its own pulse from the sound of marches.

My slippery vessel, headlong into the night—
ashore with my sleep, expecting to be gathered.

DIASPORA SONNET SENT PAR AVION WITH AN INK BLEMISH FROM A BROKEN PEN

You bit the end off the fountain pen
and blue terraced into the creases

of your neck. Seeing the ink run across
your Adam's apple to form an island there

rising at the surface of your voice—I am
dizzy. So I look away. Yet, hearing you

I know your throat rises at each swallow.
To know air like that is to write it down

and to understand belonging. I am here
and you are here. And we are separated

only by air between us—topography
traversed by my eye following the line

of dye chasing its tail from the lip edge
to the knot in a language I'd forgotten.

DIASPORA SONNET ASLEEP IN A LANDSCAPE FULL OF BLOSSOM AND NOTHING SPECIAL

Because the crocuses praise themselves
I awake from fitful sleep. I awake

next to the mountains to sheets too thin
around my ankles and to the maddening

purple of selfish blooms. Because of blooms
the mountains are all too alone and

because of their statuesque beauty,
I'm reminded of the cool hours when

what's rooted is what's presumed
of my emptied-out self. Unlike the flowers

the mountain and my own displaced
selves are tired of being lied to about comfort.

About how the sky's edges will urge me
into my own breaking. My own split pod.

DIASPORA SONNET WITH DAYTIME TV AND NOTHING ELSE

The episode was in black and white
and the waxen starlet struck a fine pose

against the window. My dreaming mother
would mimic that pose, forearm aloft, pressed

to her forehead. Was it a feigned or real
pain? Her daily quarrels with our house

were real enough—and her reckonings faint
against the rhythmic tick of static

as the rabbit ears were adjusted
for a clearer view of the cathode's beam.

Years later her lacquered hair is thin,
her wrists show blue veins as she again

models her dashing Hollywood silhouette
transposed, prolific, night against the sun.

DIASPORA SONNET IN A HOTEL PARKING LOT AT BREAK TIME

He should have stayed home. Shouldn't have moved beyond
seeing himself in mirrored storefronts, Vegas,

Rodeo Drive, the palm-lined streets of Miami
where petrichor sticks to sinuses and

where the teens in bikinis cast wide gazes.
The jobs held were about possibility.

Yet he's tired of pretending to fix
the ice machine or the blinking neon.

The schemes he's dreamed shouldn't work
and they don't—or haven't. The peeled orange

holds something bejeweled beneath, and the smell
of the peel in the car seat, sickening.

He is fragrant in the sun. The tank, full
of gas and his rind-tinged hands, going numb.

DIASPORA SONNET AS RIPPLES IN THE SNAKE RIVER

I take my name and place it on a stone.
I throw the stone into the river and watch

myself widen in circles. Who am I
to hold this world in my fist? I know what

displaces reflections on the surface.
What can't be contained edges water out.

Years later will it overrun the roots
on the shore? And what is a shore of ruins?

Will houses lean on their pilings? Mouths near
the edge of speaking? Will the waters mark

language by the rings of mold on gypsum?
Where do I begin? I told you with all

doubt cast aside. The forest roots will gnarl
in the dark. The tributaries will cough.

DIASPORA SONNET AT THE FEEDERS BEFORE THE FREEZE

I'm getting cold and the trees have darkened
into a tobacco-colored stain. Birds

cease calling each other—no more ears
in the branches. I haven't slept for two nights

because their silence skewers everything.
My thoughts cannot be broken. The depths

of my thinking sink me. I hold firm
despite the rain, its dissolution.

There are no sparrows or chickadees, they
no longer fling back their heads, exalted.

Where have they gone? The birds and the finery
of their throats? Their gratitude for seed and suet?

PANTOUM BEGINNING AND ENDING WITH AN INTERNATIONAL LUGGAGE CAROUSEL

Where do they go? Where do they come from?
These duct-taped bags. These knock-off designer cases
bound from someplace, headed toward another lap
around the ball-bearing racetrack surrounded by faces.

These duct-taped bags—these knock-off designer cases
belong to someone. Each mystery, layered with tags,
around the ball-bearing racetrack, surrounded by faces.
Names in Sharpie scrawls and "HEAVY" labels.

They belong to someone. Each mystery, layered with tags
because they are someone's burden. They are someone—
names in Sharpie scrawls and heavy labels
showing the gathering travelers a new truth. The truth?

They are someone's burden. They are someone
that has left and is forever leaving. A country. A self.
Showing the gathering travelers a new truth. A truth
in the story of a mother's lip gloss. A father's shoes

that have left and are forever leaving. A country. A self
divided into the slats of a black conveyor belt.
Each thing a story: Mother's lip gloss. Father's shoes,
their laces snared into the immigrant's story,

divided into the slats of a black conveyor belt
and bound from someplace. Headed toward another lap—
the laces snared into the immigrant's story,
Where did they come from? Where did they go?

III.

Dwelling Music

CHAIN MIGRATION III:
COIN-OP LAUNDROMAT, FRIDAY EVENING

And even when the clothes aren't dry
there are things to do:
the language lessons, muffled cries
of cycles ending. Sew

buttons on the shrunken shirts. Bear
the wailing baby up
while folding pants in tiny squares.
Then a man interrupts

your weekly chore—"You're beautiful."—
But you ignore his pass.
The timer's done. You're dutiful—
you move from task to task

because it's Friday evening. Late.
The baby's tired face,
your motivation. You collate
the shirts and then retrace

your way. Broken laundry machines
form dull aisles. Powdered soap.
The heat. The loud exhaust. The sheen
of sweat on your head. I hope

for the end of chores for all time.
A silly thought that's crossed
your brain. The dryer needs a dime.
How the evening cuts its losses

and how the quarters tumble forth
into those waiting here
for their load to be done. For birth
into the world where there

are never clothes to dry. Never
important chores undone.
Where a mother's life is leisure
with hours they've outrun.

DIASPORA SONNET IN THE MORNING

Awake with fever, ideas yammered—
little finches tearing me to dust. Mother,

awake. She prayed her gratitudes for roads
and rest stops. She counted the mile markers

fissuring the nothing hours. Driving,
country jangled and twanged glorious,

as royalty. I could not sit up or drink
because fever held me in the meanwhiles

of my skull. My tinderbox throat swollen,
holding back what it could. The old seams of

myself flexed as a needle pierces through
tissue. Mother spoke for me, breaking in

the new language. She bit. Her molars ground
down. Her false teeth sunk in their yellowed brine.

DIASPORA SONNET WITH THE PRAIRIE
HUMMING THROUGH THE SEAMS
OF A CAR DOOR

Our eyes push against the dark while boxes
swallow bones, tongues, enclose our lavish skin.

The wind flutes through cracks, high-pitched like dog whines.
All night the boxes hold us. The urge to speak.

To say anything—but to whom? Tired
of the landscape. Of being emptied. Worn

tires on the interstate, humming sounds
of treads thinning on the summer tar.

We are tired of ourselves already
in this new century, awash in smells,

a human stink with our nowheres, pungent,
stewing. A wonder we can't hold our breaths.

A wonder we can't see where we are destined,
in spite of it all. In spite of it all.

DIASPORA SONNET IMAGINING MY FAMILY'S DEPARTURE

From the archipelago a sound. It roars
with the heat of planes lifting off

the tarmac. Their broad orchestras
stretch their throats and crack the scene

in two. There is only before and after
the plane in the animal minds of birds

hurrying away from what must be
the voice of god. I'm afraid to confess

a nostalgia for the moment of their departure—
the planes and their perforation

into the sound of everything. The machines
that create the world are always for another—

from their wake, only this scar of sound
and a firmament moving on without us.

DIASPORA SONNET AS A FERRY AND ALL THAT IT CARRIES

The air by the docks smells like old batteries
and the moon rises through with its judgment,

floods the swale above the scene, and makes everything
sharp-edged. The shadows of forms more knife-like.

Each boat's prow a scythe steadily rocking,
moored and clean. The sides rub the docks,

graze of hips as lovers pass in an alley.
Some of us lose our words for such beauty. The cold

and the light and the air's insistence on us
catching our breaths having traveled on such boats

and their willful enterprise to "wherever she takes me."
The divine and stuporous words we tell ourselves

climbing out of the steerage—the rainbowed
film on waters beyond our vision.

DIASPORA SONNET WITH GRANDMOTHER'S NETTLE TEA, U.S. CITIZENSHIP PETITIONS, AND NOTHING ELSE

Nettles for tea and the sore yesteryear
awake in the old calendar whose months

have not turned—and past the steam, the ceiling
fan cuts at the syllables of story,

saying *then, then, then,* each moment of being
somewhere and someone sliced into dimes. Sugar

can make this sweet yet the bitter pinprick
keeps company. Old hymns on the radio

whittle distance. Slice after slice this tether
severed until there's nothing but tea and news

and the lying months in their effacement.
Spiral-bound but absent-minded photos,

the crossed-off days until losing count and hope.
The broth on the lips, stunned till words don't come.

DIASPORA SONNET AS A ONE-HOUR DRY CLEANER AND A FORGOTTEN CLAIM TICKET

Broth of boiled cloth and acid hands, knuckles
raw from wringing suds and swinging denim

by fistfuls up and out of the basin. Grime
of steam and grease stains blotted out. Shirt

after shirt garnished in plastic. New
selves from pressed sleeves. Starch-stiffened and formal

as one should be—in another country
I might have been royalty. Hemmed in seams

and moistened seals on thin envelopes. Wired
funds—to the Pacific from my republic

of hangers. I let hot fabrics blister
My arms. I let the dryer roar. I shout names,

perfect, sequined, and neatly pressed.
And let the plastic wrap encase each dress.

DIASPORA SONNET AS THE LAST PORTIONS AND NOTHING ELSE

These fishbones on a platter, sucked clean. More
skeletal, than sheen—blue porcelain

plates hold a carcass. And on a white dish,
boney portions. In times of famine, no

fish. Empty plates can be all colors. Small
contingencies of fact are fact. Not fat.

The fat from the eye is/was the sweetest
meat. The fried fin, eaten also. The mind

leaves nothing but numb and hind portions—tails,
the crunchy bits. Savored tilapia—

now empty portions—no rice for the bowl.
White plates bought on thrift can clatter when stacked

like decks of cards. Blue plates in the sink soak
grease. The fat from frying leaves its ghost trace.

DIASPORA SONNET IMAGINING MY FATHER ON THE INTERSTATE WITH DIVIDING LINES BLURRING BENEATH

Outside the hills are yielding mysteries
to snow. The past creases itself into

smaller and smaller blankets. How to live
your current life? Meadows open into meadows.

I've questioned the days when I can't fix things . . .
when the horizon edge never fits any

seams. I've questioned the weeks I've seen Father
wander from home to home inside the space

of a room. How to live your current life?
Road maps and gas. Packing just enough to change

from one dry shirt to another. To have enough
change for a shower and a side-road shelter.

And time to fill the dashes on asphalt
with the cursive roads, neat as yellow paint.

DIASPORA SONNET DRIVING THROUGH THE CASCADE MOUNTAINS WITH APPARITIONS

The radio does not broadcast courage.
Guardrails hold our car to the winding road.

The rearview fills with ghosts. Long black hair hangs
from their mossy heads. I see no faces.

They wait in empty bowls. They haunt the edge
of the shoulder as mile markers pass. Curves,

hairpins, deep ascending mountains. They glare
past the visor. Crosses against their chests,

they dine and wheeze past all the window seams
we've sealed with tape. Our bodies hurtling

through these overpasses hewn from deep stone.
They still whistle. They still sing through the gaps.

In the vents their reedy voices fog up
the windshield. Their names scrawled on the mirrors.

DIASPORA SONNET SURFING FOR NEWS ON THE WEB AND NOTHING ELSE

Father refreshes the browser. The ruler's
face stretched into yawn. His jeweled

incisor winks as the camera pans
past him toward the crowd. Hands

waving as the bodies turn and face
the cordoned bleachers. Confetti and lace

careening down the promenade like hail
in sudden downpours. The vehicles snail

past. Diesel belches into the brightened scene
and masses of people march in step. Careen

down the victorious streets. Loving the view
the ruler smiles and nods. He waves to a few

young boys. Father dreams he is among his flock,
stitched into storylines—weary day's shock.

DIASPORA SONNET PERSISTENT WITH GHOSTS
WHILE HUNTING PHEASANT IN ALFALFA FIELDS

My father kept his guns beneath his bed
because he thought that every knock, every

stranger at the door would be uniformed.
Some strong-armed soldier who'd come for him,

ready to "tease" out where my uncles hid.
And though we're countries, years away from there

he worries still. Imagines every fist
against the door's a hammer's violence.

Even in alfalfa fields on the banks
of the Snake River: pheasant screeches, grouse

gulps, the deep hum of a harvester, all
transform into boots, loudest above

the crack of a shotgun's declaration.
Its name in ever diminishing echoes.

DIASPORA SONNET AS MY FATHER THINKING ALOUD ABOUT THE WASTEFULNESS OF RICE TOSSED AT A WEDDING

Someone explained the blues
was a suffering from political despair.

And yet it is hard to fathom art
from the unshielded body. Handfuls

of rice tossed into the air. Arc of the grains
rain their parabolas across the sky. Father

wondered at this ritual, the waste a type
of savagery. Is this a celebration or toil?

He could never tell. And whether he sings
a type of blue note as he drives from one job

to the next, it is hard to discern the art
coming from the whistle passing between

his lips. Whether that friction and the octaves
made so sharply will ease *that* ache.

DIASPORA SONNET WITH OUR EXPECTATIONS, DECEPTIONS, AND NOTHING ELSE

We wanted to construct a livable world
but the pieces didn't fit. We wanted

the *barely there* and the *no threat to my family*.
Wanted the unaggrieved clothes of someone

who belonged. We wanted to fit under
the sweet tent by the sea. Wanted the open

screen door. There were flotillas of us, yes.
And each of us was a new acrobat

for the circus. We were jangly and beautiful,
yes. We knew the mountains posed the good

questions. We knew the midway games
were rigged. We knew the carnival barker

raised the height of the hoop slightly so
the eye would never legislate incongruity.

DIASPORA SONNET IMAGINING MY FATHER AT CAMP CRAME AGAIN, IN A LINE STRETCHED FOR A MILE

Arrow straight, a procession of men.
The line hammered into a fuse winding

from one end of the building to the other.
Gilt into a lyrical fountain, the men—

gods in another country—made small talk.
Where, after all, was there to be? And Father

among them fussed with his tie. And the dust
had its own voice which made the wait all the more

beautiful and sepia. And there were
soldiers with rifles crossing their chests because

they were the real gods here and because blood
is the quickest dialogue. The rifle,

the most honest framer. It is the firmest
maker of straight queues and straighter spines.

DIASPORA SONNET POSING AS BLOSSOMS IN LOLA'S GARDEN

Rhododendron blooms at the window,
lapping at the glass. Obscene tongues.

Their smattering of kisses in the wind,
a seasonal ache. Their leaf bobs—

the way they clasp and unclasp flowers
to mark memory and time. Rosettes,

fused mouths puckered into refusal.
Saying nothing. Breathing nothing

but their acidic earth. The loam of a place
inhospitable beneath the white pine

whose killing needles glint in shards
of dire necessity. And where flowers

bud and break, where the hummingbirds
careen, I am weary of this sharp order.

DIASPORA SONNET IN OCTOBER, AS THE MIGRATIONS BEGIN AGAIN

Chorus of uncertain pitch. Accidental
beauty adjacent to the river's throat.

The molt of too many geese and enflamed
love. The violent and seasonal riot.

Their desperate return and flight and return
to the new. How is it their atomic need

is considered welcoming? And whoever says
warmer climes look askance at the feathered

pests? Never. They're ever welcomed
as symbol to mark the passing unease.

And yet their noise is a disgruntlement. And yet
their presence is halfway banal. And yet

crossing and uncrossing the air barely coaxes
a nod or a stare or a cough. Different, as they are.

DIASPORA SONNET WITH HUNGRY GULLS AT LUNCH HOUR, DOCKSIDE

And long ago he spent the days beside
the boats. The gulls would circle, ride the currents

and shout for scraps. They pirouette and dive,
abandoning their sleeping mountain tops.

My father, with his sandwiches at lunch,
not bothered by the fury of the birds but rather

curious. Their hungers, cravings, affronts—
they bank with the oceanic gusts. Hours

too soon spent yielding to the shoreline sprays,
surrendered over to the hazardous

tilt of gull and gull-like need. Their greed
not his. He'd dream—after clocking his shift—

among the swoons of hungry, mottled heads,
holding empty plastic bags. Crusts of bread.

DIASPORA SONNET IMAGINING MY FATHER PUTTING AWAY HIS SUITS BECAUSE THERE'S NO PLACE TO GO

The fact that love was what had brought us here
still registers against my father's loss—

a pact he made when he was only years
removed from primary. And still the costs

are ghostly stops and starts that drift, amid
his daily oaths. Sometimes he'd pause to brush

the soot from cigarette ash. Formalistic
and pomaded, the straight-legged pant suit, plush

with that promise of love borne from abroad.
Such elegant clothes. The best he could pack,

and how he glistened with promise. Well-shod,
his left and right, now burdened steps. Manic

with worry, now. My beautiful father,
under the heavy calculus of what's after.

DIASPORA SONNET WITH GRANDMOTHER, HER INSOMNIA, AND NOTHING ELSE

Grandmother steeled herself around the edges
of a sound. The late-night hum of breathers,

thick, against her insomnia. Dredges
up a glimpse of somewhere. Footsteps. Nadir—

the lateness of the year affixed in zero
sleep and zero things to do. Anxious crab,

I watch her scoot across the tile. Her ears
finding my creaking step and then she'd stop

and wrestle out a pot with utmost care.
The darkness of the hours to herself,

broken with her grandson's curious stares.
She'd heat up rice and pour warm milk to soak

the troubled songs of living far away,
then drowse, upright. Untidily in place.

DIASPORA SONNET IN AUTUMN, DRIVING WEST
WITH NO PLACE TO BE

In places lodged between the pine and scrub,
my father worked in offices. He held a job

that brought him money, food, a place to sleep.
Between sleep and salt and broken floorboards

the hills off in the distance bloomed with flowers
when it rained, but often it did not. White

with frost in October, the chaparrals
gave in to interstates that disappeared—

one hill into the next and then horizon.
Between horizon and the dream of what's snow,

we resided. The road—it took him west
and east. Into the next town and the rest,

where home was just glossy book covers.
Where evening and October flickered over.

DIASPORA SONNET WITH CREOSOTE, POSTAGE, AND NOTHING ELSE

And what I remember is yellowed plains,
creosote bushes—interstate dashes

tumbling past disappearing hills. We drove
until there were no longer roads, but ships,

the jagged masts, closed-up parentheses.
It was the end of the world in my eyes—

the landscape, impossibly colorless
from the tinted car windows. Then transformed

to let the breeze in. Distant, my father,
rewritten in the annals of his book,

must have imagined his changing purpose
as America zoomed by, scrub to sea

into and out of signatures and stamps
found on the pages of what's been revised.

DIASPORA SONNET HEADING TO THE HORIZON'S EDGE ALONG I-84

Go west and west and west, they said. Mother
looking for a brute salvation, temple

steeples thrust their fists up as we pass them
on the interstate. The stratum of sky,

pressed into September. Everything hazed
into a filamentous light. Tapered,

the world zeroing in on us. Our car,
some replica of commerce—a language

we were just learning. And the dash burns hot
under the relentless and treeless plains.

West, where the idea of beauty blurs by,
filling our absences as the miles pile.

West, where the sun incandescently fades
and Mother's breath mists the glass with her sigh.

DIASPORA SONNET UNWINDING INTO THE HORIZON

In quiet spaces, there's a light you sense
upon your face. It grows there in your eye,

a kindred speechless thing, as though the stars
above the plains were prayerful from afar.

There is a thing to immigrants—a voice
they hear in brightened summer night. A call

like dusks above the meadow, woven. Fixed.
Just there above the horizon line, out

into the beyond, unwinding into ordered
hues, gradations of memory where one

belonged. More than a lifetime ago, there
in the ardor of dusk, it's there, higher

than your reach. It is the soft pad in the ear,
walking among the grasses, beyond here.

DIASPORA SONNET SPEEDING ALONG A RUNWAY, PITCHING AND ROLLING INTO SOMETHING NEW

The ocean cut the sky. The landscape, grids
below the dense plane glass. Jigsaw farms, fields

abutting the small, collapsing wave fronts.
In the beginning we were above all,

with the order of things undetermined.
History was a complication. Flight,

something beyond the world. Heartbeats, halting
in the minor turbulence. Our window

telling the story of how the world was
forming as we passed an ocean into

the mouth of a new myth. Once. Once there was—
And it came upon a runway, silvered

and sleek. Its engines held the door open,
and through the door the world tumbled away.

DIASPORA SONNET IMAGINING MY FATHER IN HIS FORTIES, WHISTLING ALOUD WITH NOTHING TO DO

My father in his fourth decade wandered
between the gaps of the haves and have nots.

We lived in a wilderness he carried,
wrapped around his shoulders, a weighted shawl

and often wondered, aloud in a flourish,
about the jet-black nights of the prairie—

how far the carbon stars wore on beyond
him. He wondered, in song, *which way the wind*

blows and I would catch him with his eyes closed,
listening to music which swelled and soared,

rebounding off the laminated floors
of the kitchen. Off in space, the cold eyes

of galaxies wondered back at him. Who
was he to question, ears to the sky?

DIASPORA SONNET AS A PHOTO OF MY FATHER, POSING NEAR THE COLUMBIA RIVER GORGE

There are rivers which always yearn to stretch
their arms into the maw of another river

and in so meeting, make another body.
My father is never happy staying

in one place. I say he is displaced
which sounds like another location

just beyond reach. He is a notion seeking
another source and yet he is aging

and his body yearns to meld into
something it will never become. Say,

American, or local. Meanwhile here
the freight boats carve grooves into the water.

What was calm lurches into an expanse—
a small tear worried into a chasm.

DIASPORA SONNET HOUSED IN THE CROOK
OF A TREE

In the sycamores, in the long hours lined
by contrails tracing back to homes somewhere,

the sky above childhood is new and large.
What's written there, for you then, disappears

Into the next town in a puff of smoke.
Or into a portion of someone's dream

perched into the crook of a tree limb, there,
enmeshed in the tangle of branches, leaves

the color of leaves. How dizzy, the self
in the tried-on selves, blending with greening

that lasted on and on despite knowing
how lost you are. How safety looks below

while the trunk sways from the added weight. You,
wanting to get away. Far from it all.

PANTOUM BEGINNING AND ENDING WITH A BIG SKY

Where the horizon meets the plains, a sharp line
cuts into my sight. Bursts of scrub and bare pine
emerge from the earth like little prayers. Unheard
breaths catch in scraps of wind. Here we are

cut into my sight. Bursts of scrub and bare pine
hold us in the frame and place us closer to home.
Breaths catch in scraps of wind. Here we are,
monuments aligned with a certain perspective.

Hold us in the frame and place us closer to home
if there's a home for us. Remember where we stand,
monuments aligned with a certain perspective—
perhaps from the side. Perhaps just disappearing.

If there's a home for us, remember where we stand
so we can return to it. Trace our steps backward,
perhaps from the side. Perhaps just disappearing
in the rearview. My father's arm on my headrest,

so he can return to it. Trace his steps backward—
back from his working paces. Back from the road
in the rearview. My father's arm on my headrest
as he puts the car in reverse. As he watches the mirror.

Back from his working paces and back from the road
I think he dreams of change. Dreams of me
as he puts the car in reverse and as he watches the mirror.
Imagines who I'd become or other possibilities.

I think he dreams of change, of me
driving out of this desert, setting fire to the road—
imagines who I'd become or other possibilities
that are, maybe, just within reach off the interstate.

I'd drive out of this desert and set fire to the road,
I'd emerge from the earth like a prayer, unheard.
I'd take the offramp and ease off the interstate.
I'd see where the horizon and the plains form a sharp line.

Acknowledgments

Grateful acknowledgment to the editors and readers of the following journals, magazines, and anthologies in which these poems first appeared, often under different titles or in different forms: *The Adroit Journal, American Poetry Review, The Baffler, Cherry Tree, Copper Nickel, Four Way Review, The Georgia Review, The Hopkins Review, Laurel Review, Literary Matters, The Los Angeles Review, The Massachusetts Review, Orion Magazine, Phi Kappa Phi Forum, The Seattle Review of Books, Shenandoah, South Dakota Review, Water~Stone Review, World Literature Today,* and *The Yale Review.*

"Diaspora Sonnet with a Death in an Apartment and the Feedback from a Radio," previously titled "Diaspora Sonnet 25," also appeared in the Academy of American Poets website, "Poem-A-Day."

"Diaspora Sonnet in the Morning Before the Rush of Crowds, When Mother Shops and Is Not Seen," previously titled "Diaspora Sonnet 40," appears in *Literature and Composition,* edited by Renee H. Shea et al. Bedford, Freeman and Worth High School Publishers, New York, 2020.

"Diaspora Sonnet Traveling Between Apartment Rentals" also appeared in the *The New York Times Magazine* in 2022.

"Diaspora Sonnet Speeding Along a Runway, Pitching and Rolling into Something New," previously titled "Diaspora Sonnet 74"; "Diaspora Sonnet Imagining My Father in His Forties, Whistling Aloud with Nothing to Do," previously titled "Diaspora Sonnet 75"; and

"Diaspora Sonnet Housed in the Crook of a Tree," previously titled "Diaspora Sonnet 76," also appear in *In the Tempered Dark*, edited by Lisa Fay Coutley. Black Lawrence Press, Mount Vernon, NY, forthcoming in 2023.

Gratitude to my friends and first readers: Rick Barot, Bruce Beasley, Mary Biddinger, Sarah Gambito, Rigoberto González, Carol Guess, Joseph Legaspi, Adrian Matejka, Erika Meitner, Aimee Nezhukumatathil, Jon Pineda, and Patrick Rosal.

Many thanks to the College of the Holy Cross and my colleagues in the English Department for cheering me on.

To Gina Iaquinta, editor extraordinaire! And to all the good people at Liveright. Thank you for believing in this book!

I am indebted to the Massachusetts Cultural Council and to the National Endowment for the Arts for their support.

To my mother, father, and grandparents. To Meredith. To Lucas, Nolan, and Henry. My unwavering love.